Sir Lancelot the Cat: A Great Soul

Katherine E. Tapley-Milton

Published by

Bruno, Saskatchewan, Canada

Sir Lancelot the Cat: A Great Soul
Written and Created by Katherine E. Tapley-Milton
Photo by Katherine E. Tapley-Milton
Cover Art by 4 Paws Games and Publishing
Edited by Katherine E. Tapley-Milton and 4 Paws Games and Publishing
Formatted and Published by 4 Paws Games and Publishing
Published 2017 First Edition
ISBN 13: 978-1-989955-03-1
Copyright © 2017 by Katherine E. Tapley-Milton All Rights Reserved
Published by 4 Paws Games and Publishing
P.O. Box 444 Humboldt, Saskatchewan, Canada S0K 2A0
http://www.4-Paws-Games-and-Publishing.ca
Publishing logo and name copyright © 2016
All Rights Reserved

The publisher is not responsible for the book, website, or social media (or its content) that is not owned by the publisher. All legal matters are to be taken up by the author as the publisher holds no responsibilities.

The author and publisher have made every effort to ensure the accuracy of the information within this book was correct at time of publication.

No part of this publication may be reproduced, distributed, or transmitted in any form or by any means, including photocopying, recording, or other electronic or mechanical methods, without the prior written permission of the publisher, except in the case of brief quotations embodied in critical reviews and certain other non-commercial uses permitted by copyright law.

Attention: Permission C/O Katherine E. Tapley-Milton 18 Squire Street Sackville, New Brunswick E4L 4K9

Table of Contents

When God Created Kitty Cats 1
In Search of a Companion 4
Street Cat 7
A Couple of Cats 12
An Old-Fashioned Remedy 13
Heavy Drugs 14
Empathy Cat 16
COMPANION by Katherine Tapley-Milton 17
Lance's Judge of Character 18
Lance's Illness 19
Epilogue 22

When God Created Kitty Cats

When God created kitty cats

He had no recipe

He knew He wanted something sweet

As sweet as sweet could be.

He started out with sugar

Adding just a trace of spice

Then stirred in drops of morning dew

To keep them fresh and nice.

He thought cats should be soft to pet

Thus, He gave them coats of fur

So, they could show they were content

He taught them how to purr.

He made for them long tails to wave

While strutting down the walk

Then trained them in meow-ology

So, they could do cat-talk.

He made them into acrobats

And gave them grace and poise.

Their wide-eyed curiosity

He took from little boys.

He put whiskers on their faces,

Gave them tiny ears for caps

Then shaped their little bodies,

To snugly fit on laps.

He gave them eyes as big as saucers

To look into man's soul

Then set a tolerance for mankind

As their purpose and their goal.

Benevolent ... and ... generous

He made so many of them.

Then charged, with Fatherly Concern,

The human race to love them.

When one jumped up upon His lap

God gently stroked its head.

The cat gave Him a kitty kiss,

"What wondrous love" God said.

God smiled at His accomplishment

So pleased with His creation

And said, with pride, as He sat back,

"At last. . .I've reached purr-fection!"

-- Author Unknown

Lance in the Living Room

In Search of a Companion

I am a freelance writer and twenty years ago I found myself living in a seedy one-room apartment in Mapleburg. I had little money and some friends in town were stressing me out. My heart was breaking because I was so lonely. There was a falling out with my family and a whole host of catastrophes that I would rather not mention. I am bipolar and suffer from OCD, and PTSD, so I struggle a lot emotionally.

What was I going to do about my forlorn state? I thought that maybe having a pet would help. I mentioned this to a friend who is a teacher, and she took me to the S.P.C.A.

I looked at every cat and kitten that they had there and none of them connected with me.

I was just about to go when I saw a spot of orange in a cage right in the very back. You are not supposed to put your finger through the bars, but I felt compelled to do so anyway. Immediately, an orange paw came out to meet my finger. I asked the staff to take this scrawny orange cat out so I could see him better.

He was rake thin and his fur was coming out in clumps. "I hope that you are not going to take that one!" my friend exclaimed.

The cat then affectionately rubbed his cheek on my hand. "Yes, I want this one!" I declared.

Driving home my friend commented "I think that you are what he needs, and he is what you need."

The S.P.C.A. insisted that I take the frail orange cat to a vet and have him neutered and declawed. I chose a vet in Lakeville, New Brunswick which was 30 minutes from my place.

I picked up the cat, who had been named "Coady" after a couple of days. He was pathetic. The vet tech said that he had a tapeworm, ear mites and fleas. He was also very groggy from the anesthetic, for days after his operations. He probably got an overdose of the drugs because he was so thin.

I cast about in my mind for a name for him, after getting him home, and suddenly I thought "Sir Lancelot!" That is what I will call him. I didn't have a real knight in shining armour, so he would be my cat in shining armour.

Lance would not eat anything for days and I was worried sick but finally the medications wore off and he took some nourishment. My friend came over and cleaned Lance's ears every day. She cleaned them so well that they never had to be done again in all of Lance's life.

My focus for a whole year after I got Lance was totally on him. We bonded very closely. When I was sick or down Lance came to my rescue and lay on my chest, looking into my eyes as if to say, "I understand mummy." There were many times when he licked tears off my cheek.

Lance in Jail

Street Cat

Lance was a street cat who was seized by the authorities because he was in such bad shape. I would wake up every morning to find my apartment was trashed. There was dirt pawed out of my plant, knick-knacks knocked over, and the fishbowl moved. Lance would look out of the patio door longingly. He wanted to get outside.

I put him in a harness and leash and took him out. Lance was not impressed. He just flopped down and refused to move. I lived on the sixth floor and when Lance knew that he was going back to the apartment he galloped up all the stairs as fast as he could.

The S.P.C.A. estimated that Lance was around two years old. He was still playful. I would throw a light-weight ball at him, and he would take it in both of his paws and bat it. Lance also loved candies that were wrapped in cellophane. He would play with a candy and then throw it over his shoulder.

One weekend I was visiting my boyfriend Dave in a city 200 miles away. I left my sister and mother in charge of Lance and my Beta fish. It wasn't long before I got a hysterical call from my sister. The fish food was missing. I always kept it right by the fish tank.

A few minutes later there was a hysterical call from my mother about the fish food. I couldn't understand why they could not find it. When I got back to the apartment, I found the can of fish food underneath a chair. Lance had been playing with it.

Christmas With an Attempted Murder

"What's this coming?" Lancelot thought. This thing that was large, green, and bushy came through the door. I yanked it with a great effort and Lancelot sniffed. It smelled of the outdoors and was prickly on his nose.

"Get out of the way of the Christmas tree!" Kathy yelled at Lancelot.

He watched with great interest as the tree was secured on a stand and given water. Lancelot lapped at the water under the tree even though he had lots of his own water in his dish.

"This thing might turn out to be fun to play with" thought Lancelot. He suddenly took a run at the tree and went straight to the top. *"Oh, what a feeling! I can see everything!"* Lancelot thought with pleasure.

Kathy then got angry and said, "You bad cat! Get down out of that tree!" Lancelot would not budge because he was a stubborn cat and liked to get his own way. Kathy got a ladder and grabbed Lancelot out of the tree.

The next morning Lancelot came out and discovered packages under the tree. He was excited and used his teeth to pull back the wrapping paper. He then found a present for himself -- a catnip mat. He rolled on it, licked it, and then lay down on it for a cat nap. He started dreaming of a forest of trees with catnip bags tied to them.

Dave and I were snowed in that Christmas, and we were under the Christmas tree together. It was then and there, in true feminist fashion, that I proposed to Dave, and he said, "yes".

When Dave came to visit, I always blew up an air mattress for him. One morning Dave woke up and couldn't breathe because his face was full of fur. Lance was blobbed on top of Dave's nose and mouth. I think that Lance was insanely jealous at that time and wanted to kill the competition for my affection.

    Dave and I went to an antique car show one summer and it rained heavily. We were tired and wet when we got home and flopped down on the bed. Dave and I were in a loving embrace and having Lance there embarrassed us both. In the end Lance came to love Dave, just as I did.

Merlin

A Couple of Cats

Every night Lance and Merlin used to have their "jousting" matches. Lance would chase Merlin one way and then Merlin would turn and chase Lance the other way. They also had World Wrestling Kitty Cat matches. Lance in his prime could flip Merlin upside down even though Merlin weighed seventeen pounds. Lance was only fourteen pounds, but after all he was a tough street fighter. On one occasion Lance was wrestling with Merlin out in the sunporch and suddenly, we heard a "biff!" as loud as if someone had been punched. Lance had socked Merlin a good one.

An Old-Fashioned Remedy

When Merlin first came to us, he had a "kitty cold" or upper respiratory infection. Lance got the cold and was extremely sick. I was scared that I was going to lose him. The vet had him on antibiotics and she loaned me her own vaporizer for Lance. Lance, however, did not like the vaporizer and hid from it. The antibiotics did not seem to help him at all. He was not eating, and his breathing was very labored. Lance went into hiding and that was when I really knew he was sick. I thought that he was crawling off to die.

My friend was a country girl and told me to mix up a cup of cream, one egg and a small capful of Brandy. I was told to syringe it down Lance's throat. I was desperate! I mixed the ingredients up and Dave held Lance. I shot some of the boozy remedy down Lance's throat. Lance came downstairs out of his sick room not too long after that, with a jaunty look on his face and his tail up. He started to get better from that moment on. I've had vets tell me that alcohol is poison to cats, but all I know is that this old-fashioned remedy with Brandy saved Lance's life.

Heavy Drugs

Every summer I grew catnip for Lance. He loved it and if I put a leaf on the floor, he slapped his paw on it as if to say "Mine!" I always put the catnip in a hanging basket because the black and white cat that used to come around ate an entire plant. We never saw him around anymore after that. Did he party hardy and die? I guess that we will never know.

I picked, on one occasion, all the blossoms off the catnip plants and put them in Lance's catnip mat that I had sewed for him. Lance was in his own "opium den" all night and at six o'clock in the morning he bit my nose hard. Blood was flying everywhere. I called the provincial nurse and she said that I had to go to the emergency department. She told me that they had to report every animal bite to the provincial vet. The emergency department doctor warned me that my nose might get deformed unless I took antibiotics. The drugs were as big as horse pills.

The provincial vet had been trying to reach me and when he got me on the phone he said, "I hear that you have an animal bite".

I exclaimed, "I gave my own tabby cat too much catnip and he bit my nose. It was my own fault."

The vet seemed satisfied with my explanation of events and the matter was closed. Later, I read that the potency of the plant goes to the blossoms of the catnip. I had been scared that they were going to put Lance down, but it turned out all right. My nose recovered and I learned not to put catnip blossoms in Lance's mat.

My Dear Boy

Empathy Cat

Sir Lancelot was always a very affectionate, empathetic cat. When I found him at the shelter and he was so sick, he was still this way. One day I was depressed and suicidal. I took a knife in my hands and was ready to cut my wrists. Lance immediately jumped up in my lap and he tried to stop me from cutting myself by pushing my hand with his cheek. When I got fired from my job, I lay on the bed sobbing and Lance came and licked the tears off my cheek. I know some people would say that he wanted the salt, but with Lance it was always about showing love and empathy.

His favorite position was on top of my chest as I lay on my back. Lance would purr and look right into my soul, so it seemed. I was given a new antidepressant one time and it made me very nauseous and weak. I lay on the couch, and I was in misery. Lance came over to the couch and took charge of the situation as he snuggled right next to me and leant me his strength. He always came to me when I was in distress, in some cases even before I knew that I was in bad shape.

The bond between Lance and I was so strong that when I would go out, Lance would plaintively howl until I got back home. When I was at Yale University participating in a clinical trial of *Transcranial Magnet Stimulation*, I was gone for month. Lance was howling every day. We could make long distance phone calls for free, so I would talk to Dave every night. I had to talk to Lance too of course. Lance was so intelligent that he recognized my voice and stopped his howling. On the ward, if I got a phone call, the patients would yell "Lance is calling!"

One of the men on the ward commented "Look at yourself! You're in a psychiatric ward talking to your cat on the telephone."

COMPANION by Katherine Tapley-Milton

An understanding

between man and beast,

We cuddle together

on interminable wet Sundays

or frigid winter nights.

While I read, he purrs

in contented feline bliss.

Head on my sneaker

 and body curled close.

Some inexplicable bonds

keeping the different two species

in a quiet, gentle intimacy.

(That poem was written about Lance.)

Lance's Judge of Character

Sir Lancelot was a good judge of character. We were dealing with a vet who abused her staff out back. She was always hyper, and Lance tried to bite her. She jumped away, otherwise she would have had a nasty wound. He also put up a terrific fight when she tried to handle him. When we went to a nice calm vet Lance behaved very well and that vet told me later that Lance definitely was special. One time my sister was not feeling well, and she lay on my couch covered up with a duvet. It was not long before Lance cuddled up to her chest and comforted her. He knew that she loved animals.

One of the obscenest things that a guy I knew did was to squeeze Lance's genitals. It's a wonder Lance did not try to bite him. I know that I was outraged. Lance and I concurred on most things.

Lance Meditating

Lance's Illness

Lance was losing weight and not looking well so I took him to the vet. They did some blood tests and told me that Lance had hyperthyroidism. Cats never get hypothyroidism like dogs they said and to cope with giving Lance the thyroid medication I got pill pockets for him. They are like little pockets where you place the pill inside the hole, and they taste like treats. Lance loved them. I would yell, "Pill for kitter!" and he would come galloping to get his "treat."

The vet had told me Lance would only last three or four years past his diagnosis. I guess that I pushed that out of my mind because Lance meant so much to me. He did do well for at least four years after his diagnosis of hypothyroidism. Lance started losing weight again and when he had some bloodwork done it was evident that his thyroid was abnormally high. I was faithfully giving him his pills, but it did not seem to help. Most disturbing of all was that he started sleeping in the litter boxes. I took a cardboard box and put blankets in it and took some waterless shampoo and tried to clean him off. I then placed Lance in a clean bed. He stayed there all the time and wouldn't eat. I had a can of sardines and as a last resort tempted him with that. He showed some interest and ate some.

One day I could not even get Lance to eat the sardines. The reality of losing him crashed in on me. I got my husband, and we went to the vets to have Lance put down. We did the worst thing possible by staying and watching him die. I stayed because I thought that Lance might need me there. The vet said, "No more pain." Then she gave Lance a lethal injection. His eyes were half open, and his body was motionless. Dave and I left the vets crying our eyes out.

I cried for weeks and was inconsolable after I lost Lance. It was as if I had lost a part of myself. I now have seven wonderful cats, but I do not have the same deep empathy that Lance showed me. Lance was selfless and noble. He was a great soul with the heart of a lion.

Lance in the Library

Lance in Heaven with Baby Skunks and the Mama Skunk

Lance in Heaven Playing with the Baby Skunks

Epilogue

Katherine E. Tapley-Milton has found ways to deal with her grief. She immortalized Sir Lancelot by writing this book and a children's story book entitled, "The Adventures of Sir Lancelot the Cat."

www.ingramcontent.com/pod-product-compliance
Lightning Source LLC
Chambersburg PA
CBHW041813040426
42450CB00001B/30